POPULAR SONGS

HAL LEONARD
TUDENT PIANO LIBRARY

G000297308

f5 **Today**

Arranged by Mona Rejino

CONTENTS

ISBN-13: 978-1-4234-0832-1

HAL•LEONARD®
CORPORATION

7777 W. BLUEMOUND RD. P.O. BOX 13819 MILWAUKEE, WI 53213

Visit Hal Leonard Online at
www.halleonard.com

Bless The Broken Road

Words and Music by Marcus Hummon,
Bobby Boyd and Jeff Hanna
Arranged by Mona Rejino

find ___ true love _____ a - long the bro - ken road. ___ But

I got lost ___ a time __ or two, __ wiped my brow __ and kept push - in' through. __

I could - n't see ___ how ev - er - y sign _____ point - ed straight __ to you. __

___ But ev - er - y long lost ___ dream __

___ led me to where you _____ are. ___ Oth - ers who broke my ___ heart, ___

3

lov - er's _____ arms. _____ This much I know _____ is _____

true: _____ that God blessed __ the bro -

- ken road _____ that led me straight _____ to you. _____

rit.

(1'48")

5

Breakaway

from THE PRINCESS DIARIES 2: ROYAL ENGAGEMENT

Words and Music by Bridget Benenate,
Avril Lavigne and Matthew Gerrard
Arranged by Mona Rejino

CODA

break - a - way.

Out of the dark - ness and in - to the sun. But I won't for - get the

place I come from. I got - ta take a risk. Take a chance. Make a change and

break - a - way, break - a -

way, break - a - way.

mf

mp *rit.* *p*

(2'54")

Don't Know Why

Words and Music by Jesse Harris
Arranged by Mona Rejino

Drops Of Jupiter

(Tell Me)

Words and Music by Pat Monahan, Jimmy Stafford,
Rob Hotchkiss, Charlie Colin and Scott Underwood
Arranged by Mona Rejino

Moderately ($\quad = 80$)

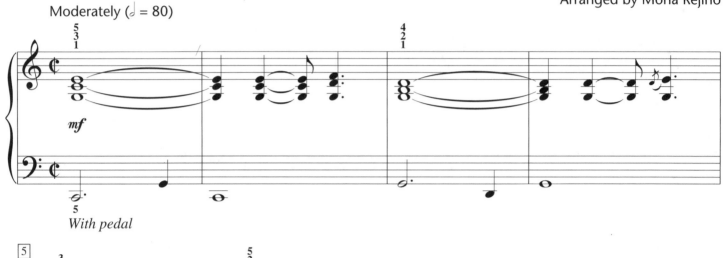

With pedal

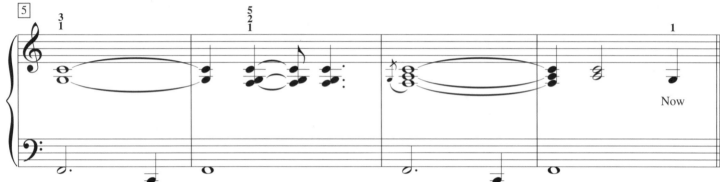

Now

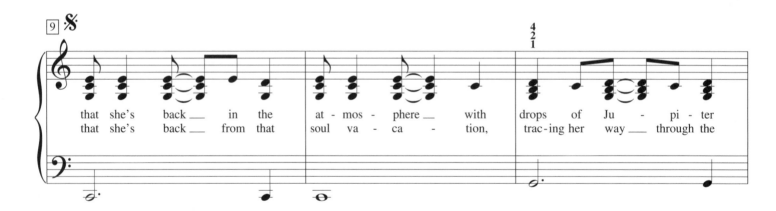

that she's back ___ in the at - mos - phere ___ with drops of Ju - pi - ter
that she's back ___ from that soul va - ca - tion, trac-ing her way ___ through the

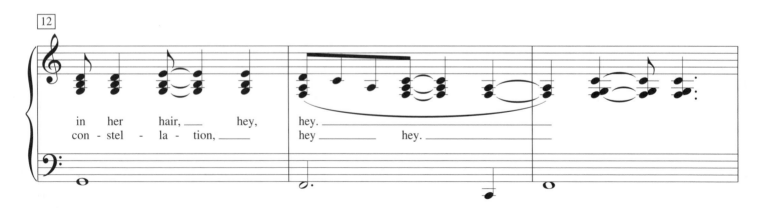

in her hair, ___ hey, hey. hey ___ hey.
con - stel - la - tion, ___ hey ___ hey.

She acts like sum - mer and
She checks out Mo - zart while she

walks like rain, __ re - minds me that __ there's a time to change, hey
does Tae - Bo, __ re - minds me that _____ there's room to grow, __ hey

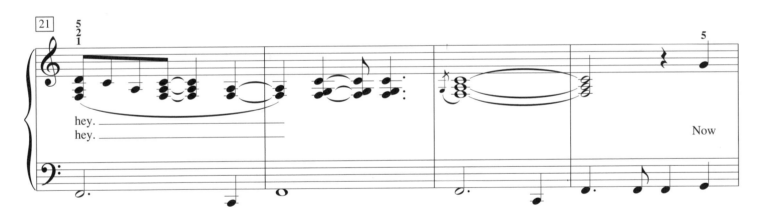

hey. __
hey. __

Now

Since the re - turn __ from her stay on the moon __ she lis - tens like spring __ and she
that she's __ back __ in the at - mos - phere I'm a - fraid that she might __ think of

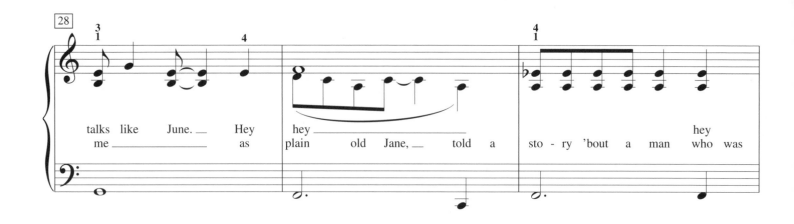

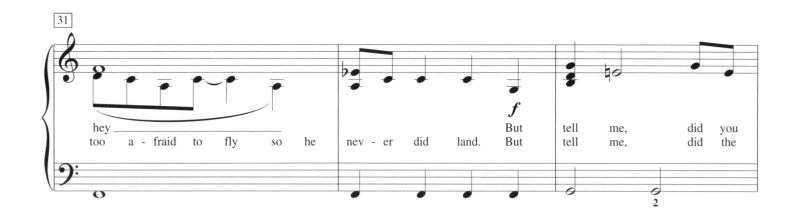

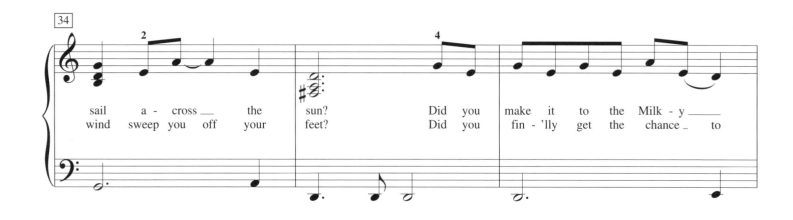

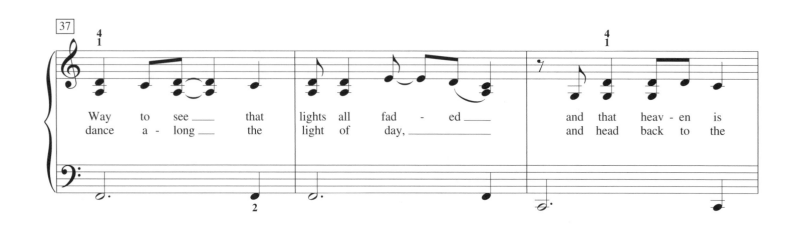

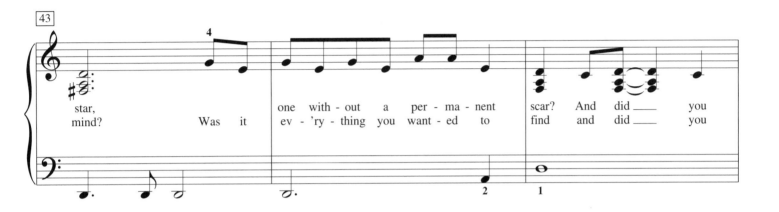

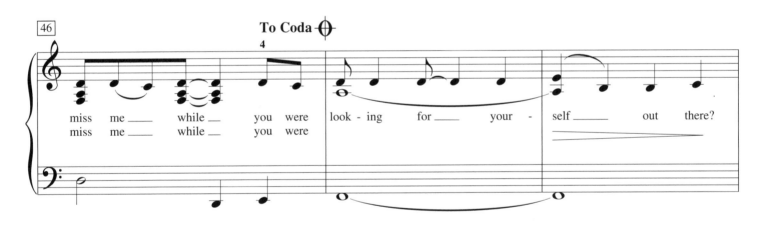

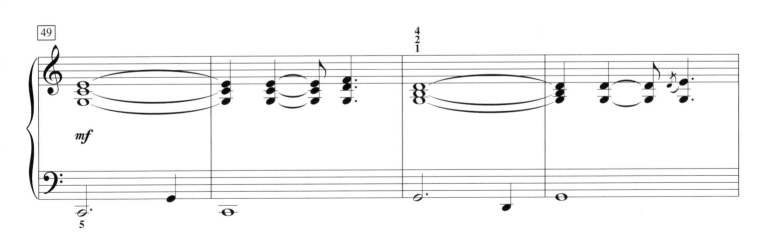

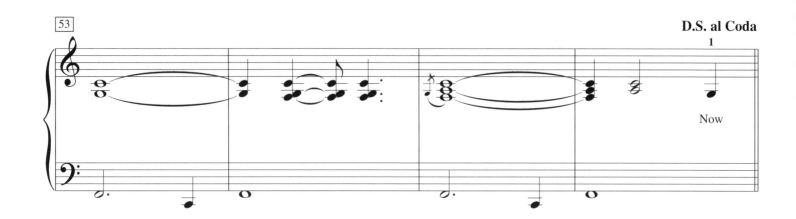

Now

CODA

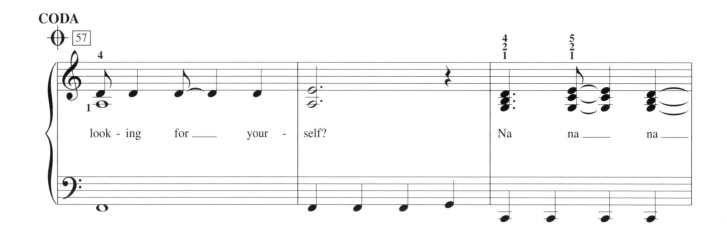

look - ing   for ____ your - self?   Na   na ____   na ____

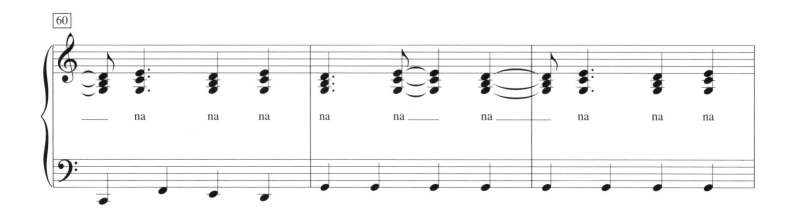

____ na   na   na   na   na   na ____   na   na   na

na   na   na   na. ____ And did you fin - 'lly get the chance to   dance a - long ____ the light of

Home

Words and Music by Amy Foster-Gillies,
Michael Buble and Alan Chang
Arranged by Mona Rejino

still feel all a - lone, __ just wan - na go home. Oh, I miss you, you

know. I've been keep - ing all ___ the let - ters ___ that I
feel just like ___ I'm liv - ing ___ some - one

wrote to you, __ each one a line or two, __ "I'm fine, ba - by,
else - 's life. __ It's like I just stepped out - side __ When ev - 'ry - thing was

how are you?" __ I would send them, but __ I know that it's __ just
go - ing right. __ And I know just why __ you could not come __ a -

not e - nough. __ My words were cold and flat, __ and you de - serve
long with me: __ this __ was not your dream, but you al - ways be -

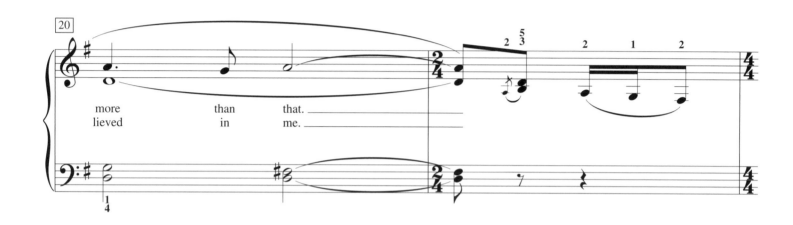

more than that. _____
lieved in me. _____

An-oth-er ae-ro-plane, an-oth-er sun-ny place; I'm luck-y, I know, but I wan-na go
An-oth-er win-ter day has come and gone a-way in ei-ther Par-is or Rome, but I wan-na go

To Coda ⊕

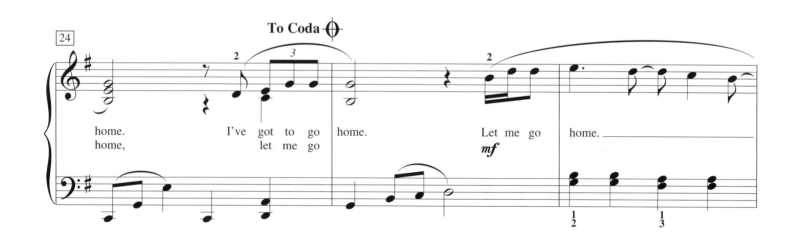

home. I've got to go home. Let me go home. _____
home, let me go

22

I'm just too far from where you are; I wan-na go

home.

D.S. al Coda

And I

CODA

home.

And I'm sur-round-ed by a mil-lion peo-ple; I, I still feel a-lone, and let me go

23

A Thousand Miles

Words and Music by Vanessa Carlton
Arranged by Mona Rejino

Moderately fast ($\quarternote$ = 92)

Mak - in' my way down - town,

walk - in' fast, fac - es pass and I'm home - bound.

If I could fall into the sky, do you think time would pass me by? 'Cause you know I'd walk a thou - sand miles if I could just see

poco a poco dim.

Listen To Your Heart

Words and Music by Per Gessle
and Mats Persson
Arranged by Mona Rejino

Some-times I won-der if this
fight is worth-while. ___ The pre-cious mo-ments are all lost in the tide, ___ yeah. ___
They're swept a-way ___ and noth-ing is what it seems. ___ The feel-ing of be-
long-ing ___ to your dreams ___
Lis-ten to your heart ___ when he's

poco a poco cresc.

(2'51")

She Will Be Loved

Words and Music by Adam Levine
and James Valentine
Arranged by Mona Rejino

Moderately (♩ = 100)

mp

With pedal

Beau - ty queen of   on - ly eight - een.
Tap on my win - dow,   knock on my ___ door.

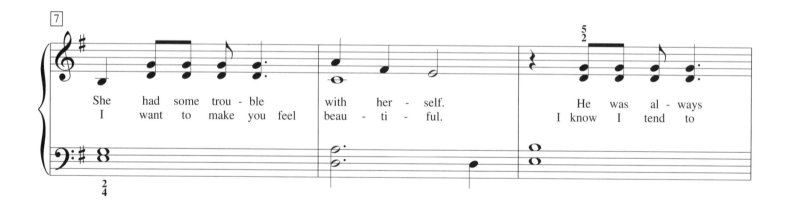

She had some trou - ble   with her - self.   He was al - ways
I want to make you feel   beau - ti - ful.   I know I tend to

there to help her. She al - ways be - longed to   some - one else.
get so in - se - cure. Does - n't mat - ter   an - y - more.

Ask her if she wants to stay a - while ___ and she will ___

To Coda ⊕

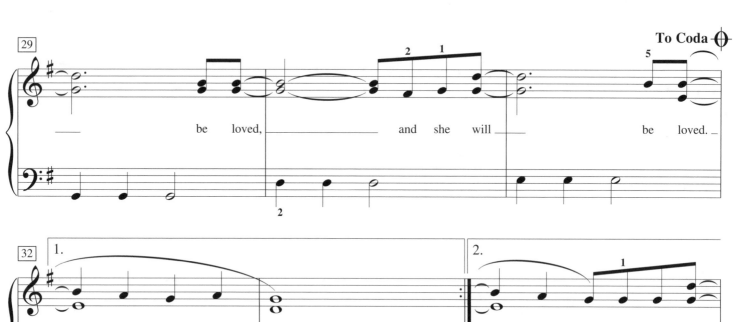

be loved, ___ and she will ___ be loved. ___

1. ___
2. ___ And she will ___

be loved. And she will ___ be loved. ___

I know where you hide ___ a - lone in your car.

Know all of the things _____ that make you who you are. _____ I know that good-bye _____

_____ means noth - ing at all. _____ Comes back and begs me, catch her ev - 'ry time she

falls, _____ yeah. _____ Tap on my win - dow,

D.S. al Coda

knock on my door. I want to make you feel beau - ti - ful.

CODA

_____ And she will _____ be loved.

(4'19")

POPULAR SONGS

HAL LEONARD STUDENT PIANO LIBRARY

The Hal Leonard Student Piano Library has great songs, and you will find all your favorites here: Disney classics, Broadway and movie favorites, and today's top hits. These graded collections are skillfully and imaginatively arranged for students and pianists at every level, from elementary solos with teacher accompaniments to sophisticated piano solos for the advancing pianist.

The Beatles
arr. Eugénie Rocherolle
Intermediate piano solos. Songs: Can't Buy Me Love • Get Back • Here Comes the Sun • Martha My Dear • Michelle • Ob-La-Di, Ob-La-Da • Revolution • Yesterday.
Correlates with HLSPL Level 5.
00296649 ....$9.95

Broadway Hits
arr. Carol Klose
Early-intermediate/intermediate piano solos.
Songs: Beauty and the Beast • Circle of Life • Do-Re-Mi • It's a Grand Night for Singing • The Music of the Night • Tomorrow • Where Is Love? • You'll Never Walk Alone.
Correlates with HLSPL Levels 4/5.
00296650 ....$6.95

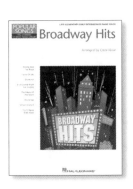

Christmas Cheer
arr. Phillip Keveren
Early intermediate level. For 1 Piano/4 Hands.
Songs: Caroling, Caroling • The Christmas Song • It Must Have Been the Mistletoe • It's Beginning to Look like Christmas • Rudolph the Red-Nosed Reindeer • You're All I Want for Christmas.
Correlates with HLSPL Level 4.
00296616 ....$6.95

Christmas Time Is Here
arr. Eugénie Rocherolle
Intermediate level. For 1 piano/4 hands.
Songs: Christmas Time Is Here • Feliz Navidad • Here Comes Santa Claus (Right Down Santa Claus Lane) • I'll Be Home for Christmas • Little Saint Nick • White Christmas.
Correlates with HLSPL Level 5.
00296614 ....$6.95

Disney Favorites
arr. Phillip Keveren
Late-elementary/early-intermediate piano solos. Songs: Beauty and the Beast • Circle of Life • A Dream Is a Wish Your Heart Makes • I'm Late; Little April Shower • A Whole New World (Aladdin's Theme) • You Can Fly! • You'll Be in My Heart.
Correlates with HLSPL Levels 3/4.
00296647 ....$9.95
Disney characters and artwork © Disney Enterprises, Inc.

Visit our web site at
www.halleonard.com/hlspl.jsp
for all the newest titles in this series and other books in the Hal Leonard Student Piano Library.

Getting to Know You – Rodgers & Hammerstein Favorites
Illustrated music book. Elementary/late elementary piano solos with teacher accompaniments. Songs: Bali H'ai • Dites-Moi (Tell Me Why) • The Farmer and the Cowman • Getting to Know You • Happy Talk • I Whistle a Happy Tune • I'm Gonna Wash That Man Right Outa My Hair • If I Loved You • Oh, What a Beautiful Mornin' • Oklahoma • Shall We Dance? • Some Enchanted Evening • The Surrey with the Fringe on Top.
Correlates with HLSPL Level 3
00296613 ....$12.95

Movie Favorites
arr. Fred Kern
Early-intermediate/intermediate piano solos.
Songs: Forrest Gump (Feather Theme) • Hakuna Matata • My Favorite Things • My Heart Will Go On • The Phantom of the Opera • Puttin' On the Ritz • Stand by Me.
Correlates with HLSPL Levels 4/5.
00296648 ....$6.95

Sounds of Christmas (Volume 3)
arr. Rosemary Barrett Byers
Late elementary/early intermediate level. For 1 piano/4 hands. Songs: Blue Christmas • Christmas Is A-Comin' (May God Bless You) • I Saw Mommy Kissing Santa Claus • Merry Christmas, Darling • Shake Me I Rattle (Squeeze Me I Cry) • Silver Bells.
Correlates with HLSPL Levels 3/4.
00296615 ....$6.95

Today's Hits
arr. Mona Rejino
Intermediate-level piano solos. Songs: Bless the Broken Road • Breakaway • Don't Know Why • Drops of Jupiter (Tell Me) • Home • Listen to Your Heart • She Will Be Loved • A Thousand Miles.
Correlates with HLSPL Level 5.
00296646 ....$6.95

You Raise Me Up
arr. Deborah Brady
Contemporary Christian favorites. Elementary-level arrangements. Optional teacher accompaniments add harmonic richness. Songs: All I Need • Forever • Open the Eyes of My Heart, Lord • We Bow Down • You Are So Good to Me • You Raise Me Up.
Correlates with HLSPL Levels 2/3.
00296576 ....$7.95

Prices, contents and availability subject to change without notice.
Prices may vary outside the U.S.

FOR MORE INFORMATION, SEE YOUR LOCAL MUSIC DEALER,
OR WRITE TO:

HAL•LEONARD®
CORPORATION
7777 W. BLUEMOUND RD. P.O. BOX 13819 MILWAUKEE, WI 53213

COMPOSER SHOWCASE

HAL LEONARD STUDENT PIANO LIBRARY

This series showcases the varied talents of our **Hal Leonard Student Piano Library** family of composers.

Here is where you will find great original piano music by your favorite composers, including Phillip Keveren, Carol Klose, Jennifer Linn, Bill Boyd, Bruce Berr, and many others. Carefully graded for easy selection, each book contains gems that are certain to become tomorrow's classics!

EARLY ELEMENTARY

JAZZ PRELIMS
by Bill Boyd
HL00290032   12 Solos.......................$5.95

ELEMENTARY

JAZZ STARTERS I
by Bill Boyd
HL00290425   10 Solos.......................$6.95

LATE ELEMENTARY

CORAL REEF SUITE
by Carol Klose
HL00296354   7 Solos.........................$5.95

IMAGINATIONS IN STYLE
by Bruce Berr
HL00290359   7 Solos.........................$5.95

JAZZ STARTERS II
by Bill Boyd
HL00290434   11 Solos.......................$6.95

JAZZ STARTERS III
by Bill Boyd
HL00290465   12 Solos.......................$6.95

MOUSE ON A MIRROR & OTHER CONTEMPORARY CHARACTER PIECES
by Phillip Keveren
HL00296361   5 Solos.........................$6.95

PLAY THE BLUES!
by Luann Carman (Method Book)
HL00296357   10 Solos.......................$7.95

SHIFTY-EYED BLUES – MORE CONTEMPORARY CHARACTER PIECES
by Phillip Keveren
HL00296374   5 Solos.........................$6.95

TEX-MEX REX
by Phillip Keveren
HL00296353   6 Solos.........................$5.95

THE TOYMAKER'S WORKSHOP
by Deborah Brady (1 Piano, 4 Hands)
HL00296513   5 Duets........................$5.95

TRADITIONAL CAROLS FOR TWO
arr. Carol Klose (1 Piano, 4 Hands)
HL00296557   5 Duets........................$6.95

*For a full description and songlist for each of the books listed here, and to view the newest titles in this series, visit our website at **www.halleonard.com***

EARLY INTERMEDIATE

CHRISTMAS FOR TWO
arr. Dan Fox (1 Piano, 4 Hands)
HL00290069   4 Medley Duets $6.95

EXPEDITIONS IN STYLE
by Bruce Berr
HL00296526   11 Solos.......................$6.95

EXPLORATIONS IN STYLE
by Bruce Berr
HL00290360   9 Solos.........................$6.95

FANCIFUL WALTZES
by Carol Klose
HL00296473   5 Solos $7.95

JAZZ BITS (AND PIECES)
by Bill Boyd
HL00290312   11 Solos.......................$6.95

MONDAY'S CHILD
by Deborah Brady
HL00296373   7 Solos.........................$6.95

PORTRAITS IN STYLE
by Mona Rejino
HL00296507   6 Solos.........................$6.95

THINK JAZZ!
by Bill Boyd (Method Book)
HL00290417.....................................$9.95

WORLD GEMS
arr. Amy O'Grady (Piano Ens./2 Pianos, 8 Hands)
HL00296505   6 Folk Songs $6.95

INTERMEDIATE

AMERICAN IMPRESSIONS
by Jennifer Linn
HL00296471   6 Solos $7.95

ANIMAL TONE POEMS
by Michele Evans
HL00296439   10 Solos $6.95

CHRISTMAS JAZZ
arr. Mike Springer
HL00296525   6 Solos.........................$6.95

CONCERTO FOR YOUNG PIANISTS
by Matthew Edwards (2 Pianos, 4 Hands)
HL00296356   Book/CD......................$16.95

DAKOTA DAYS
by Sondra Clark
HL00296521   5 Solos.........................$6.95

FAVORITE CAROLS FOR TWO
arr. Sondra Clark (1 Piano, 4 Hands)
HL00296530   6 Duets........................$6.95

JAZZ DELIGHTS
by Bill Boyd
HL00240435   11 Solos.......................$6.95

JAZZ FEST
by Bill Boyd
HL00240436   10 Solos.......................$6.95

JAZZ SKETCHES
by Bill Boyd
HL00220001   8 Solos.........................$6.95

JEROME KERN CLASSICS
arr. Eugénie Rocherolle
HL00296577   10 Solos....................$12.95

LES PETITES IMPRESSIONS
by Jennifer Linn
HL00296355   6 Solos.........................$6.95

MELODY TIMES TWO
arr. Eugénie Rocherolle (2 Pianos, 4 Hands)
HL00296360   4 Duos (2 Scores).......$12.95

POETIC MOMENTS
by Christos Tsitsaros
HL00296403   8 Solos.........................$7.95

ROMP!
by Phillip Keveren
(Digital Ensemble/6 Keyboards, 6 Players)
HL00296549   Book/CD......................$9.95
HL00296548   Book/GM Disk $9.95

SONGS WITHOUT WORDS
by Christos Tsitsaros
HL00296506   9 Solos.........................$7.95

SOUNDS OF CHRISTMAS
arr. Rosemary Barrett Byers (1 Piano, 4 Hands)
HL00296406   5 Duets........................$6.95

SOUNDS OF CHRISTMAS, VOL. 2
arr. Rosemary Barrett Byers (1 Piano, 4 Hands)
HL00296529   5 Duets........................$6.95

THREE ODD METERS
by Sondra Clark (1 Piano, 4 Hands)
HL00296472   3 Duets $6.95

THE TWELVE DAYS OF CHRISTMAS
by Deborah Brady
HL00296531   13 Solos $6.95

FOR MORE INFORMATION, SEE YOUR LOCAL MUSIC DEALER, OR WRITE TO:

HAL•LEONARD® CORPORATION
7777 W. BLUEMOUND RD. P.O. BOX 13819 MILWAUKEE, WI 53213

Prices, contents & availability subject to change without notice.

0705